Papatango Theatre Compa

The world premiere of the
2016 Papatango New Writi

ORCA
by Matt Grinter

First performance at Southwark Playhouse, London:
Wednesday 2 November 2016

ORCA

by Matt Grinter

Cast in order of speaking

Fan	**Carla Langley**
Maggie	**Rona Morison**
Joshua	**Simon Gregor**
Gretchen	**Ellie Turner**
The Father	**Aden Gillett**

Director	**Alice Hamilton**
Designer	**Frankie Bradshaw**
Lighting Designer	**Johanna Town**
Music and Sound	**Richard Hammarton**
Producer	**Chris Foxon**
Dramaturg	**George Turvey**
Casting Director	**Emily Jones**
Fight Director	**Tim Klotz**
Accent Coach	**Hugh O'Shea**
Production Manager	**Ian Taylor**
Costume Supervisor	**Flora Moyes**
Stage Manager	**Roisin Symes**
Design Assistant	**Jasmine Swan**

Cast and Creative Team

Aden Gillett | The Father

Aden won the Off West End Award for Best Actor for *Accolade*.

Theatre includes *R and D* and *Amongst Friends* (Hampstead); *A Midsummer Night's Dream* (Shakespeare's Globe); *The White Carnation, Accolade* (Finborough); *The Doctor's Dilemma* (National Theatre); *Next Time I'll Sing to You* (Orange Tree); *The Little Hut* (UK tour); *The Price* (Edinburgh Lyceum); *Mary Poppins* (Prince Edward); *Much Ado About Nothing, Design for Living* (Theatre Royal Bath); *Blithe Spirit* (Savoy/tour); *Betrayal* (Duchess/tour).

Film includes *A Caribbean Dream, You Will Meet a Tall Dark Stranger, Tula: The Revolt, Collusion, The Winslow Boy*.

Television includes *Vera, Father Brown, Holby City* (series regular Edward Campbell), *Silk, The Impressionists, The Queen's Sister, Pollyanna, Innocents, Ivanhoe, The House of Eliott, Harry Enfield's Television Programme*.

Simon Gregor | Joshua

Simon trained at RADA.

Theatre includes *American Psycho, The Late Henry Moss, The Hypochondriac* (Almeida); *Around the World in 80 Days* (St James); *A Midsummer Night's Dream, Things We Do for Love, King Lear* (Theatre Royal Bath); *Widowers' House* (Orange Tree); *To Kill a Mockingbird, Much Ado About Nothing* (Regent's Park); *The Taming of the Shrew, Pericles, The Tempest* (RSC); *Uncle Vanya* (Arcola); *Chekhov in Hell* (Drum Theatre Plymouth); *The Miser* (Royal Exchange Theatre, Manchester); *The 39 Steps* (Criterion); *Interior, Red Demon, Beauty and the Beast* (Young Vic); *The Lion King* (Royal Lyceum); *Snake* (Hampstead); *The 39 Steps, Marat/Sade, Wild Honey, Happy Haven* (West Yorkshire Playhouse); *Gas Station Angel* (Royal Court); *The Front Page* (Donmar Warehouse); *Full Moon* (Theatr Clwyd/Young Vic); *Master Harold and the Boys* (Contact, Manchester); *Mabingo* (Moving Being); *Weldon Rising* (Royal Court/Liverpool Playhouse); *Woman in Mind* (Windsor Theatre Royal); *Damned for Despair, Three Judgments in One* (Gate); *Good Person in Setzuan* (National Theatre); *Inventing a New Colour* (Royal Court/Bristol Old Vic); *Privates on Parade* (Bolton Octagon); *Catch-22* (Dukes Lancashire); *The Marriage of Figaro* (Theatr Clwyd).

Film includes *Welcome to the Punch, A Casualty of War, Bodywork, Escape from Sobibor, Last Seduction II, The Island on Bird Street, The Statement, The Wrong Blonde, Young Toscanini*.

Television includes *Harry Price: Ghost Hunter, Apocalypse Slough, The Borgias, Da Vinci's Demons, Holby City, Ripper Street, Black Mirror: The National Anthem, MI High, King James Bible, New Tricks, Doctor Who, 20 Things to Do Before You're 30, Arabian Nights, Avarice, Blag, Drop the Dead Donkey, Love on a Branch Line, Men Behaving Badly, Mine All Mine, Mersey Beat, Queen of Clubs, Swallow, The Bill, The Keep, Waking the Dead*.

Carla Langley | Fan

Carla graduated from drama school in 2012. She won the 2016 Manchester Theatre Award for Best Studio Performance, and was nominated for Best Female Performance at the Off West End Awards for *Cuddles*.

Theatre includes *Future Conditional* (Old Vic); *Cuddles* (New York/Ovalhouse/tour); *The Minotaur* (Polka/Theatr Clwyd); *Liolà* (National Theatre); *Desolate Heaven* (Theatre503); *The Three Lives of Lucie Cabrol* (Edinburgh Fringe Festival); *As You Like It* (Sam Wanamaker Festival, Shakespeare's Globe).

Television includes *Witness for the Prosecution, Penny Dreadful*.

Rona Morison | Maggie

Rona trained at Guildhall.

Theatre includes *Julie* (Northern Stage); *The Crucible* (Bristol Old Vic); *Scuttlers* (Royal Exchange Theatre, Manchester); *The James Plays* (National Theatre); *To Kill a Mockingbird* (Regent's Park); *Crave and Illusion* (Bush/tour); *Anhedonia* (Royal Court); *The Second Mrs Tanqueray* (Rose, Kingston); *Buckets* (Orange Tree).

Film includes *Ready Player One, Love Bite, The Boy I Loved, Sliding*.

Television includes *Decline and Fall*.

Ellie Turner | Gretchen

Ellie won the 2014 Golden Egg Film Festival Award for *Black Cab* and received Ian Charleson Award Commendations in 2010 and 2013.

Theatre includes *R and D* (Hampstead); *Hamlet, The Cherry Orchard* (National Theatre); *Stone Face, Merit, Drama at Inish, Hindle Wakes* (Finborough); *Nordost* (Salisbury Playhouse/Egg, Bath); *Bloody Poetry* (White Bear); *School for Wives* (Upstairs at the Gatehouse); *Oliver Twist* (Riverside Studios); *La Ronde, The Playboy of the Western World, Henry V* (Riverside Studios/tour); *Avocado* (King's Head); *Alphabetical Order* (The Mill at Sonning).

Film includes *How You Look At Me, Black Cab, Silence, TV Audioville*.
Television includes *Misfits*.

Matt Grinter | Playwright

Matt lives in Bristol. He worked as a director prior to beginning a career as a writer. His very first play, *Angel*, was produced by Papatango in 2008 and won the Lost Theatre's One Act Play Festival; this inspired Matt to focus on his writing. His second play, *The Dog and the Elephant*, had short runs at the VAULT Festival and the Bristol Old Vic Studio, where he is currently one of the Open Session Writers on attachment. *Orca* will be his first full production.

Alice Hamilton | Director

Theatre as director includes *German Skerries* (Orange Tree/tour); *Eventide* (Arcola/tour); *Visitors* (Bush/Arcola/tour); *Orson's Shadow* (Southwark Playhouse); *Fear of Music* (Up in Arms/Out of Joint tour), *Missing* (Tristan Bates); *At First Sight* (Latitude Festival/tour).

Alice worked as Staff Director on *Man and Superman* at the National Theatre, and has directed development workshops and rehearsed readings with the Royal Court, National Theatre, Salisbury Playhouse, and HighTide. She is co-artistic director of Up in Arms.

Frankie Bradshaw | Designer

Theatre as designer includes *Adding Machine* (Finborough); *Clickbait, A First World Problem* (Theatre503); *Barbarians* (Young Vic; JMK Award 2015, Olivier Award nominated); *Grav* (Torch Theatre, Wales); *Stories from the Sea* (Unity, Liverpool); *Punk Rock* (Actor's Studio, Liverpool); *The Picture of Dorian Gray*, *The Comedy of Errors* (LIPA, Liverpool).

Site-specific work includes co-designing *Karagula* (STYX, Tottenham) and *If Walls Could Talk: 100 Seel Street* (Seel Street, Liverpool). Frankie has also designed the Young Vic's *5 Plays 5 Days* and *Fresh Direction* projects and has worked as associate designer to Christopher Oram on many productions including *The Winter's Tale, Harlequinade, Romeo and Juliet* and *The Entertainer* (Garrick); *Man and Superman* (National Theatre); *Photograph 51* (Noël Coward); *Hughie* (Booth, New York), and *Damsel in Distress* (Chichester Festival Theatre). Frankie was a Linbury Prize finalist in 2015 working with the Lyric Theatre, Belfast.

www.frankiebradshawdesign.com

Johanna Town | Lighting Designer

West End and international credits include *Dear Lupin, Fences, What the Butler Saw, Some Like It Hip Hop, Betrayal, Speaking in Tongues, Beautiful Thing* (West End); *Rose* (National Theatre/Broadway); *My Name is Rachel Corrie* (Royal Court/West End/New York); *Guantanamo* (New York/Tricycle/ West End); *Arabian Nights, Our Lady of Sligo* (New York); *Haunted* (Royal Exchange Theatre, Manchester/New York/Sydney Opera House); *The Steward of Christendom* (Out of Joint/Broadway/ Sydney); *Macbeth* (Out of Joint/world tour); *The Permanent Way* (Out of Joint/National Theatre/Sydney); *Our Country's Good* (Out of Joint/Toronto/USA).

Other theatre includes numerous productions for the National Theatre, Chichester Festival Theatre, Sheffield Crucible, English Touring Theatre, Royal Exchange Theatre, Manchester, and over 50 productions for the Royal Court. She is an Associate Artist for Theatre503 where credits include *The Life of Stuff* (Off West End Award nomination for Best Lighting Designer).

Opera includes *Porgy & Bess* (Royal Danish Opera); *Rinaldo* (Estonian National Opera); *Carmen, Kátya Kabanová* (Scottish Opera).

Johanna is an Honorary Fellow at Guildhall School of Music and Drama.

Richard Hammarton | Music and Sound

Theatre includes *Girls* (HighTide Festival/Soho); *Burning Doors* (Belarus Free Theatre); *Much Ado About Nothing, Jumpy* (Theatr Clywd); *After Independence* (Papatango at Arcola); *Linda* (Royal Court); *Tomcat* (Papatango at Southwark Playhouse); *The Crucible, Brilliant Adventures, Edward II, Dr Faustus* (Royal Exchange Theatre, Manchester); *A Number* (Nuffield/Young Vic); *Crushed Shells and Mud* (Southwark Playhouse); *Comrade Fiasco* (Gate); *Grimm Tales 2* (Bargehouse, Oxo Tower Wharf); *Beached* (Marlowe/Soho); *The Pitchfork Disney, Ghost from a Perfect Place* (Arcola); *The Crucible* (Old Vic); *Dealer's Choice* (Royal & Derngate); *Kingston 14* (Theatre Royal Stratford East); *Sunspots, Deposit, Fault Lines* (Hampstead); *Early Days (of a Better Nation)* (Battersea Arts Centre); *Sizwe Bansi is Dead, Six Characters Looking for an Author* (Young Vic); *The Taming of the Shrew* (Shakespeare's Globe), *Speaking in Tongues* (Duke of York's); *A Raisin in the Sun* (Lyric Hammersmith/ national tour); *The Last Summer* (Gate, Dublin); *Mudlarks* (HighTide Festival/ Theatre503/Bush); *Ghosts* (Duchess); *Judgement Day* (The Print Room); *Persuasion, The Constant Wife, Les Liaisons Dangereuses, Arsenic and Old Lace, The Real Thing, People at Sea* (Salisbury Playhouse); *Platform* (Old Vic Tunnels); *Pride and Prejudice* (Theatre Royal Bath/national tour); *Dealer's Choice* (Birmingham Rep); *Hello and Goodbye, Some Kind of Bliss* (Trafalgar Studios); *Breakfast with Mugabe* (Theatre Royal Bath); *Someone Who'll Watch Over Me* (Theatre Royal Northampton); Olivier Award-winner *The Mountaintop, Inches Apart, Ship of Fools, Natural Selection, Salt Meets Wound* (Theatre503).

Television includes *Ripper Street, Agatha Christie's Marple, No Win No Fee, Sex 'N' Death, Wipeout, The Ship*.

Orchestration includes *Agatha Christie's Marple, Primeval, Dracula, Jericho, If I Had You, A History of Britain, Silent Witness, Dalziel and Pascoe, Alice Through the Looking Glass, The Nine Lives of Tomas Katz, Scenes of a Sexual Nature*.

Interactive and digital work includes *You Shall Go To The Ball* (Royal Opera House); *Light* (BAC); *Foundling Museum* (The Foundling Museum, London); *Moore Outside* (Tate Britain/Coney).

Chris Foxon | Producer

Chris joined Papatango in 2012 and his productions with the company include *After Independence* (Arcola); *Tomcat* (Papatango New Writing Prize 2015, Southwark Playhouse); *Coolatully* (Papatango New Writing Prize 2014, Finborough); *Unscorched* (Papatango New Writing Prize 2013, Finborough); *Pack, Everyday Maps for Everyday Use* (Papatango New Writing Prize 2012, Finborough). His other productions include *The Transatlantic Commissions* (Old Vic); *Donkey Heart* (Old Red Lion/Trafalgar Studios); *The Fear of Breathing* (Finborough; transferred in a new production to the Akasaka Red Theatre, Tokyo); *The Keepers of Infinite Space* (Park); *Happy New* (Trafalgar Studios); *Tejas Verdes* (Edinburgh Festival); *The Madness of George III* (Oxford Playhouse).

Chris is a visiting lecturer at the Royal Central School of Speech and Drama and the University of York.

George Turvey | Dramaturg

George co-founded Papatango in 2007 and became the sole Artistic Director in January 2013. He trained as an actor at the Academy of Live and Recorded Arts (ALRA) and has appeared on stage and screen throughout the UK and internationally, including the lead roles in the world premiere of Arthur Miller's *No Villain* (Old Red Lion/Trafalgar Studios) and *Batman Live World Arena Tour*. Credits as director include *After Independence* (Papatango at Arcola); *Leopoldville* (Papatango at Tristan Bates); *Angel* (Papatango at the Pleasance London and Tristan Bates). As a dramaturg, he has led the development of all of Papatango's productions.

Emily Jones | Casting Director

Theatre as casting director includes *Donkey Heart* (Old Red Lion/Trafalgar Studios); *Coolatully* (Papatango at Finborough); *World Enough & Time* (Park); *The Hard Man* (Finborough); *The Keepers of Infinite Space* (Park); *Unscorched* (Papatango at Finborough).

Television as casting director at the BBC includes *Doctors*.

As an assistant Emily has worked at the BBC on *Silent Witness, Father Brown, Casualty, The Coroner* and *Doctors,* and in theatre with Ginny Schiller on various projects including *The Father* (Theatre Royal Bath/West End); *1984* (West End/various tours); *Bad Jews* (Theatre Royal Bath/West End); *The Merchant of Venice* (Almeida); *Pride and Prejudice* (Regent's Park); *Fatal Attraction* (Theatre Royal, Haymarket).

Tim Klotz | Fight Director

Tim trained at Bristol Old Vic and qualified with Fight Directors Canada and British Academy of Dramatic Combat. He has been a specialist fight director and combat tutor for over twenty years. Tim has also been resident fight director at Drama Centre London/UAL for the past decade. This summer Tim was on the Faculty for the World's Stage Combat Teacher's Conference, after serving on the World's Stage Combat Certification Conference academic committee since 2013.

Theatre includes *Troilus and Cressida* (Shakespeare's Globe); *Romeo and Juliet* (Haymarket, Basingstoke); *Alpha Beta* (Finborough); *Robin Hood, Treasure Island* (Tobacco Factory, Bristol); *Warriors Experience* (Madame Tussauds).

Ballet includes *Romeo and Juliet, Peter Pan, Robin Hood* (Nashville Ballet).

Film includes *Cockneys vs Zombies, Cinderella* (performance), *Fisticuffs, Invisible, Callum, Rage.*

Television includes *James May's Man Lab, Falling Apart, Conquest, Privates.*

Video Games include *Killzone 2, Shellshocked 2, Rome Total War, Medieval Total War 2.*

Tim has spent the last two years as a development consultant to British Fencing, developing alternate fencing for youth and higher education.

Hugh O'Shea | Accent Coach

Theatre includes *The Maids, Doctor Faustus, The Commitments* (Jamie Lloyd Company/ATG); *Bugsy Malone, Herons, Cinderella, Tipping the Velvet* (Lyric Hammersmith); *Pride and Prejudice* (Sheffield Crucible); *Breaking the Code* (Royal Exchange Theatre, Manchester); *The Odyssey* (Liverpool Everyman); *Oh What a Lovely War* (ATG); *The Light of Heart* (Clwyd Theatr Cymru); *Uncle Vanya* (St James); *In the Heights* (Southwark Playhouse).

Television includes *Happy Valley, Peaky Blinders, Nigel Farage Gets His Life Back, Houdini and Doyle, Vera, The A Word, Home Fires, The Last Kingdom.*

Film includes *HHHH, One United, Churchill, The Jungle Book.*

Hugh has taught at the Royal Central School of Speech & Drama, LAMDA, ALRA, Rose Bruford and the Identity School of Acting.

Flora Moyes | Costume Supervisor

Flora trained at Nottingham Trent University.

Theatre includes *Adding Machine* (Finborough); *Karagula* (STYX); *Landgirls , French Fancies* (Swank Street Theatre), and *Mrs Hudson's Christmas Corker* (Wilton's Music Hall).

Film includes *The Heresy of Champna.*

Production Acknowledgements

Papatango New Writing Prize 2016 Reading Team | **Joanna Bobin, Michael Byrne, Harriet Creelman, Charlie de Bromhead, Sam Donovan, Karis Halsall, Ellie Horne, Jonny Kelly, Justine Malone, Deirdre O'Halloran** and **Matt Roberts**

Image Design | **Rebecca Maltby**

Production Photography | **The Other Richard**

Press Representation | **Kate Morley PR**

Orca was originally developed by Papatango with the following cast:
Ellie Bamber, Pearl Chanda, Rosie Day, Paul Hamilton and John Mackay.

Huge thanks to our post-show event contributors Kim Barker, Leigh-Ann Hale, Sophia Kingshill, Doc Rowe, Robert Stanex, Noreen Tehrani, and The Folklore Society.

Many thanks also to Arts Council England, Backstage Trust, Boris Karloff Charitable Foundation, Bristol Old Vic, Derek Hill Foundation, Garfield Weston Foundation, Old Vic New Voices, James Peries, Royal Victoria Hall Foundation, and Kathryn Thompson.

BackstageTrust www.docrowe.org.uk

'Remarkable unearthers of new talent' *Evening Standard*

Papatango Theatre Company was founded in 2007 to find the best new talent in the UK with an absolute commitment to staging their work. We provide opportunities for those otherwise unlikely to break into theatre.

Papatango have produced or developed new plays from emerging playwrights across the UK, and our discoveries have been produced worldwide.

The Papatango New Writing Prize was launched in 2009, offering a four-week production, publication by Nick Hern Books, and a commission for a follow-up play. The Prize is unique in UK theatre. No other annual opportunity guarantees a full production and publication to, nor commits to such long-term development of, a new writer.

Moreover, every script we receive (over 1500 in 2016) gets personal feedback. This reflects the company's mission to encourage all new talent and launch brilliant new theatre-makers with the greatest possible impact.

2015 Prize-winner James Rushbrooke is developing his play *Tomcat* for television and became a writer on attachment at the Old Vic. He was nominated for the Off West End Award for Best New Play. 2014 Prize-winner Fiona Doyle's second play *Deluge* premiered at Hampstead Theatre. She then joined the National Theatre Studio on attachment.

2013 Prize-winner Luke Owen's *Unscorched* transferred to the Milano Playwriting Festival, Italy. 2012 Prize-winner Louise Monaghan has produced work with Octagon Theatre Bolton and BBC Radio 4. Tom Morton-Smith, writer of our runner-up play *Everyday Maps for Everyday Use* in the same year, saw his play *Oppenheimer* produced by the Royal Shakespeare Company and transfer to the West End.

Other Prize-winners include Dominic Mitchell, who won two BAFTAs for his BBC series *In The Flesh*, having been discovered and championed by Papatango who produced *Potentials*, his debut show. Dawn King's *Foxfinder* was one of the Independent's Top Five Plays of the Year and won Dawn the OffWestEnd Award for Most Promising Playwright and the inaugural National Theatre Foundation Playwright Award, as well as the Critics' Circle Most Promising Newcomer Award for director Blanche McIntyre. Dawn and Blanche then collaborated on *Ciphers* with Out of Joint.

In 2014 Papatango established the Resident Playwright position. Our inaugural Resident, May Sumbwanyambe, went on to be commissioned by National Theatre Scotland and Radio Four, and our production of his play *After Independence* at the Arcola Theatre was critically acclaimed. In 2015 Samantha Potter became Resident Playwright and won a bursary from the Channel 4 Playwrights' Scheme with Papatango. In 2016 our Resident Playwright is Sam Grabiner.

Papatango run an extensive programme of free playwriting workshops in schools and community centres, reaching over 1000 individuals so far in 2016. All our opportunities are free and entered anonymously, encouraging the best new talent regardless of means or connections.

Papatango are a registered charity. We operate without core funding and rely on the generous support of individuals as well as trusts and foundations to deliver our unmatched programme of world premieres from brilliant new writers who would otherwise go unseen. We use the success of our discoveries to inspire others that they too can break into theatre. All you need is a story...

Please do consider helping us to find, develop and stage these stories.

If you would like to support Papatango or perhaps get involved in a particular project, then please email **chris@papatango.co.uk.**

We make a little go a long way. Did you know that:

£5 buys a ticket for an in-need young person

£10 covers the cost of printing scripts for an entire cast

£20 funds a free place at a community playwriting workshop

£50 provides 25 free playtexts for school libraries

£75 pays for a day of rehearsals

£100 provides a full costume for a character on stage

£200 enables us to travel to run workshops across the UK

£500 pays for a special performance for a school group

£1000 funds a week of script R&D with actors and writer

£2000 supports a budding writer with a seed commission

£6000 commissions a full script from a new writer

£10,000 supports a cast of 5 for a month-long show

Every donation makes an enormous difference.

Online
For up-to-date news and opportunities please visit:
www.facebook.com/pages/PapaTango-Theatre-Company/257825071298
www.twitter.com/PapaTangoTC
www.papatango.co.uk

Papatango Theatre Company Ltd is a registered charity and a company limited by guarantee. Registered in England and Wales no. 07365398. Registered Charity no. 1152789.

'Southwark Playhouse churn out arresting productions at a rate of knots' *Time Out*

Southwark Playhouse is all about telling stories and inspiring the next generation of storytellers and theatre-makers. It aims to facilitate the work of new and emerging theatre practitioners from early in their creative lives to the start of their professional careers.

Through our schools work we aim to introduce local people at a young age to the possibilities of great drama and the benefits of using theatre skills to facilitate learning. Each year we engage with over 5,000 school pupils through free schools performances and long-term in school curriculum support.

Through our participation programmes we aim to work with all members of our local community in a wide ranging array of creative drama projects that aim to promote cohesion, build confidence and encourage a lifelong appreciation of theatre.

Our theatre programme aims to facilitate and showcase the work of some of the UK's best up and coming talent with a focus on reinterpreting classic plays and contemporary plays of note. Our two atmospheric theatre spaces enable us to offer theatre artists and companies the opportunity to present their first fully realised productions. Over the past 23 years we have produced and presented early productions by many aspiring theatre practitioners many of whom are now enjoying flourishing careers.

'A brand as quirky as it is classy' *The Stage*

For more information about our forthcoming season and to book tickets visit www.southwarkplayhouse.co.uk. You can also support us online by joining our Facebook and Twitter pages.

ORCA

Matt Grinter

Characters

FAN, *fourteen*
MAGGIE, *eighteen*
JOSHUA, *fifty-two*
GRETCHEN, *sixteen*
THE FATHER, *sixty-two*

This text went to press before the end of rehearsals and so may differ slightly from the play as performed.

Scene One

Overlooking the harbour.

FAN *sits on empty lobster pots, looking out eagerly. At her feet are jam jars and candles. She places the candles in the jam jars and ties a length of rope around the top of them, placing them along the quayside.* MAGGIE *is sat away; she is distant. She reads a book and is deep in thought.*

FAN. My skin is hard and white and cold… (*Waits.*) My voice is a rumble deep and old… Maggie?… Maggie! My voice is a –

MAGGIE. You're Dad's boat.

FAN. Oh.

MAGGIE. You did that one last week.

FAN. It's your turn then.

MAGGIE. Maybe later, Fan.

FAN. Come on.

MAGGIE. I'm busy.

FAN. You're not busy, I'm busy, we're both supposed to be making the lanterns. And I have to dance for the fishermen tonight, and I have a thousand things to do before I'm ready. The dress needs altering and I have to pick up my flower garland. (*Beat.*) Do you think if our da was The Father, The Father of the whole village, I'd still have to dance or would I just be crowned The Daughter without all the fuss.

MAGGIE. Our da could never be The Father. Only fishermen can become The Father.

FAN. I don't mind, I want to dance.

MAGGIE. Can we talk about something else?

FAN. Not unless you have a riddle!

FAN *grins mischievously at* MAGGIE *who rolls her eyes.*

MAGGIE. My skin is rough and worn, my eyelids flutter, my thoughts are black on white –

FAN. It's your book, it's always your book. You're not even trying.

MAGGIE *looks up from her book.*

MAGGIE. Alright… My belly swells, my skin she bellows, in time my bright-blue eyes turn to yellow…

FAN (*screws up her nose, thinking hard*). Is it a bruise, you did that one when I knocked my shins tripping over the workbench.

MAGGIE. It wasn't a book though was it, now let me read.

FAN. But it's not a new one, a hard one. If you aren't going to help with the lanterns you could at least think of a new riddle.

MAGGIE. Alright, I'll think, just give me some quiet please.

FAN *thinks silently and her attention is drawn out to sea.*

FAN. Can you see the boats coming back yet?

MAGGIE. You won't see them from here.

FAN. I might.

FAN *looks on, staring harder into the distance, she places a newly finished lantern on the ground.*

We could run to the wall, I bet we'd see them there.

MAGGIE. Not today, Fan.

FAN. Then when? We could see them from the wall I'm sure.

MAGGIE. You have to finish the lamps and I have to watch over you. Watching for the boats won't make the day go any faster, it'll just mean we won't get the lamps done and then we'll both get it.

FAN *reluctantly returns to her lamps.*

FAN. They're just fiddly is all, and I don't see the point of the
    lamps anyway? Ma said it was to guide them home but the
    fishermen do that journey every day, in fog or rain or... They
    know their way back to the harbour...

MAGGIE. It used to be, they used to guide them home, now it's
    for fun, for decoration. So fiddly or not you better get a move
    on with them or there won't be any lights for the party later.

    Beat.

FAN. It'd go quicker if you helped.

MAGGIE. I'm not helping.

FAN. Please, Maggie.

MAGGIE. I told you I'm not –

FAN. You don't have to come tonight, it would just be the lamps.

MAGGIE. Listen, it's not that I don't want to help you –

FAN. Please?

MAGGIE. I tell you what. If you can finish them quickly we
    might have time for lunch on the harbour, then we can lay
    out the lamps along the wall and look out for the boats.

    FAN *smiles.*

FAN. And when they come back from fishing we can start, we
    can start getting ready for the dance, we can pick up my
    garland and you'll braid my hair?

MAGGIE. Don't push it.

FAN. No one braids my hair as pretty as you, Da's got fat fingers!

MAGGIE. We won't have time to –

FAN. Please!

MAGGIE. Fan – (*Beat.*) don't put all your hopes on being
    picked, the village... The Father... we're not... they
    wouldn't pick us, not now, not our family, I don't want you
    getting upset.

She notices FAN's *crestfallen face.*

Alright, little Fan, I'll braid your hair, if you promise you'll not mention the dance every time you draw a breath?

FAN *is overjoyed.*

FAN. Of course.

MAGGIE. Of course.

FAN *grins and starts preparing the remaining lamps.*

FAN. I want to look beautiful when we dance, I want to look like a mermaid.

MAGGIE. Fan –

FAN. Tonight I'll look beautiful and I shall ask The Father to dance with me.

MAGGIE. You can't just march up to him and ask him to dance.

FAN. Why not? Da said The Father works for us, he keeps us safe and leads the fishing boats and –

MAGGIE. It doesn't work like that. He's busy, speaking with the council, the other fishermen, he'll have too much to do on a day like this to worry about dancing with the likes of you. You should stay away from him.

FAN *thinks.*

FAN. The bells, Maggie, why do they ring the warning bell, at the festival. When the ships go out with The Daughter?

MAGGIE. To remember her sacrifice, to remember the sacrifice of all we've lost to the sea.

FAN. And is it the actual real Daughter's boat from the story?

MAGGIE. So they say.

FAN. So it's hundreds of years old? Did it feel… safe, when you were The Daughter?

The question hangs for a moment in the air. JOSHUA *strides on the stage. He is a carpenter. He is a small man, pale and wan, as if the joy and the strength have been washed from*

*him. He is grey and thin, not in any way physically
threatening. He is the girls' father. He strides purposefully
past* FAN, *ruffling her hair as he passes, and heads to*
MAGGIE.

Da!

We see now his rage. He grabs MAGGIE *by the dress and
pulls her to her feet. It is a hollow gesture despite his rage,
a man struggling to assert himself.*

JOSHUA. You'll not make a mockery of me, girl, not here.
Christ can you not keep your lips together!

FAN *runs to* MAGGIE *and tries to pull her from her father.*

Do you hear me? Maggie, lies! Again your lies!

FAN. Da, stop!

JOSHUA. Maggie! Do you understand, girl? Do you hear me?

FAN. She hears you, Da, let go of her, you're ripping her dress.

JOSHUA. I want her to say it.

MAGGIE. I hear you.

JOSHUA *lets her go and walks away, his rage subsiding
slightly.* FAN *looks to* MAGGIE. MAGGIE *is calm.*
JOSHUA *looks back to his girls.*

JOSHUA. I won't have this any more, Maggie, I won't... ah,
for Christ's sake, Maggie, don't stand there saying nothing.

MAGGIE *rolls her eyes and remains silent, calmly picking
up her book.*

You can't carry on like that around the village, you can't...
flapping your tongue, spilling that bile! You know how hard
it's been, for all of us, and you have a mind to make it all
worse... Maggie!

MAGGIE. Of course, Da.

JOSHUA *sits, the fight seems to be leaving him somewhat.
He glances at* MAGGIE *and* FAN, *who is still holding her
sister.*

JOSHUA (*to* FAN). Oh girl, come here… come here.

MAGGIE. Go and see your da.

FAN *starts to separate herself from* MAGGIE.

FAN. You shouldn't pull at her, you shouldn't.

JOSHUA. Don't you start with your sister's lip, my list of shouldn'ts is half the length of hers and I'm twice her age… Why do you do it, Maggie?

MAGGIE. What was it this time?

JOSHUA. Don't you give me that, girl, you were heard.

MAGGIE. Heard? By who?

JOSHUA. By Clem, in the village, talking shite!

FAN. What shite?

JOSHUA. Language, Fan!… And that's not the half of it.

FAN. Half of what?

JOSHUA. The flowers, telling Clem we didn't have the money, that we –

MAGGIE. I said nothing to Clem.

JOSHUA. Do you have any idea how people see us, what people would think, I've saved for months for that garland –

FAN. The flowers for the garland, Maggie? You know I can't dance without them.

JOSHUA. What did you think would happen, save for spoiling the day for your little sister?

MAGGIE. I didn't say anything to Clem, Da.

JOSHUA. You were seen at his store, Maggie!

MAGGIE. I was… I went there, to the shop but –

JOSHUA. Damn it, girl, you heap lies on top of lies until you'll sink us all!

MAGGIE. I said nothing, believe what you will.

JOSHUA. I will at that! Don't talk at me as if I'm witless, I'm no fool.

MAGGIE. I have to, Da, you don't catch on if I complicate it –

JOSHUA *stands and makes to go for her again.* FAN *throws herself between them.*

FAN. MAGGIE!

MAGGIE. Let him come, Fan.

JOSHUA. Take that back, girl, or I swear...

MAGGIE. Why would you believe a word I say, if I did half the things the village accused me of I'd need forty arms and as many days in a week, I was never there!

JOSHUA. Out of my way, Fan.

FAN. Stop it, both of you stop it. The boats.

JOSHUA. Move, Fan!

FAN. Da, please, the boats!

JOSHUA *turns to his younger daughter.*

JOSHUA. What boats, what boats, Fan? You can't see them from here.

FAN. Listen.

The sound of a bell off in the distance rings out, all three stop to listen to it. The mood changes. JOSHUA *and* MAGGIE *turn to look at each other.*

MAGGIE. The bells...

FAN. They're too early.

MAGGIE. No, Fan, it's not for the dance, someone's hurt.

JOSHUA. Shit... Shit! Maggie, take your sister and run to the house, get the table ready. Whoever it is, whoever they bring, lay them downstairs and get things ready like Dr Macauley showed you. I'll run and fetch him.

FAN. Do you think they're alright?

MAGGIE. We don't know yet. Now come on, we can finish these later.

FAN. Will they still have the party?

MAGGIE. Fan!

JOSHUA. Take her back now, and boil some water, they'll need boiled water.

JOSHUA *looks to* MAGGIE, *for a moment worried.*

Marcus said he saw the pod yesterday afternoon, from the wall… saw the orcas…

MAGGIE. It's nothing, Da, it's superstition, stories.

JOSHUA. Let us hope so.

He goes to leave and stops, looking back at MAGGIE.

MAGGIE. Go and get the doctor, Da.

JOSHUA *leaves.* MAGGIE *and* FAN *hurriedly pick up the things they have been using to make the lanterns and thrust them into* MAGGIE's *bag.*

Blackout.

Scene Two

JOSHUA's *workshop.*

The lights come up on a bare workshop, a table stands near a window on the right-hand side. On the table is laid GRETCHEN. *Young and gaunt, she is a ghost of a girl. She's unconscious. Sat near her, watching her, is* FAN, *she doesn't take her eyes from the table. Across the room,* MAGGIE *busies herself preparing the room for the doctor. She fetches rags, prepares a bowl of boiled water and tidies the space near the table.*

FAN. Do you think she'll wake?

MAGGIE. I don't know.

FAN. How do you think she got out there?

MAGGIE. I don't know, Fan! You've been with me the whole time, I know the same as you know.

FAN. Do you think she's a mermaid? I think she's a mermaid. A mermaid that gave up her tail to come and live on the land... Maybe for love?

MAGGIE. It's Gretchen, Evvie Miller's daughter, from the other side of the island, she's not a mermaid, Fan.

FAN. But maybe... Maybe she saw someone, from within the waves, and so she came to shore to find him.

MAGGIE. She's a fisherman's daughter, like everyone else round here, don't let your head go wandering off or else you're like to get it bashed.

FAN *stares at* MAGGIE *for a moment.* FAN *waits, watching* MAGGIE, *testing the water. Tentatively she tries again.*

FAN. Maybe she's –

MAGGIE. FAN!

Beat.

FAN. Do you think she is hurt because they saw the pod?

MAGGIE. It's nothing to do with the orcas.

FAN. Are you sure? They frighten me, the orcas.

MAGGIE. I'm sure.

FAN. The last time the pod was seen the little Thompson boy drowned.

MAGGIE. It's nonsense.

FAN. The time before that –

MAGGIE. If you aren't going to help me will you at least be quiet, Da will be here with the doctor any minute and we're not nearly ready.

Beat.

MAGGIE *begins to lay out the doctor's medical instruments from the bag he has left.*

FAN. Will you still braid my hair?

MAGGIE *looks at* FAN *but says nothing.*

I'd like you to. I think I should surely get picked if you were to –

MAGGIE. Stop it, Fan.

FAN. Stop what? Why do you hate them all so, you shouldn't hate the village, The Father. He looks after us all, he's kind, he's –

MAGGIE *snaps at* FAN.

MAGGIE. Fan, will you be quiet!

MAGGIE*'s anger is short-lived and she softens when she sees her sister recoil.*

If the wind changes!

FAN. What?

MAGGIE. The wind she blew about the place and stuck her with her sour face!

FAN *is still stinging from the rebuke*.

FAN. You talk a lot of nonsense, Maggie, more than me, more than all my talk of... you talk a lot of nonsense.

Beat.

MAGGIE *can see her sister is hurt, she stops what she is doing for a moment*.

MAGGIE. I have one for you.

FAN. One what.

MAGGIE. A riddle.

FAN. Really! Is it new, is it hard?

MAGGIE. Very new, very hard. Listen carefully... and think, don't say the first thing that rushes into your mind... The Devil smiled and marvelled this, 'How loud, how vile silence is.'

FAN *thinks hard*.

FAN. Um... the warning bell, no, no a...

MAGGIE. Come on.

FAN. The Devil?

MAGGIE. Think about it.

Suddenly GRETCHEN *sits bolt upright and shouts. They all scream and* FAN *runs behind* MAGGIE. GRETCHEN *looks around her, terrified. She tries to stand, knocking a bowl to the floor. Stood for a moment, she looks at the girls and at her surroundings, then her weakened legs buckle beneath her*.

GRETCHEN. Legs...

GRETCHEN *collapses on to the floor and passes out again. Both girls stand shocked*.

FAN. Is she dead?

MAGGIE. I don't think so.

She runs to her, checking her pulse.

She's fine, she's weak, passed out again I think.

FAN. Did you hear what she said!

MAGGIE. I did, Fan, but –

FAN. Legs, she said legs like she… Like she'd never seen them before.

MAGGIE. Fan!

FAN. Like she didn't know how to use them and she just, she fell…

MAGGIE. She said legs, Fan, because they stopped working, now get over here and help me, for Christ's sake.

FAN runs over to help her sister and looks in newfound awe at GRETCHEN. They pull her towards the table and lay her on the floor near it.

Run and look out for Da and the doctor, tell them that the girl is waking and they need to come quickly.

FAN. But I want to stay with the mermaid!

MAGGIE. Go quickly, she's stirring.

FAN reluctantly runs from the room. MAGGIE fetches the bowl and fills it full of water from the jug. She grabs a cloth and walks towards GRETCHEN.

She kneels next to her on the floor and begins to mop her brow. After a while GRETCHEN stirs again, she starts and tries to sit up and MAGGIE jumps back from her. They stare at each other. MAGGIE smiles gently.

Gretchen, can you hear me? You were found, by our fishermen, in the ocean. You were found and brought here and we've cared for you. You've nothing to fear here. It's me, Maggie, my father is Joshua, the carpenter, Joshua. He's gone to fetch the doctor to look you over.

GRETCHEN *looks around the room confused and then back to* MAGGIE.

We're the closest house to the harbour; if anyone is injured, anything terrible happens at sea they ring the bells, they bring them here first. The doctor keeps a bag, some supplies, at our house... Are you thirsty?

GRETCHEN *hesitates for a moment and then she nods.*

You're safe now, don't be afraid, you're safe.

She nods again, and MAGGIE *stands and moves to the jug.*

My da will be here any minute.

She pours her a glass of water and hands it to her. GRETCHEN *drinks and looks at* MAGGIE.

You're Gretchen, Evvie's daughter, aren't you?

GRETCHEN *is silent. She stares at* MAGGIE, *still unsure what to make of her surroundings. She is still terrified.*

You've nothing to fear here, I promise you. You're safe here, Gretchen, you're back on the island, back at the village.

This seems to upset her. GRETCHEN *has begun to shake, holding the glass of water, she starts to sob, desperately, panicked.* MAGGIE *is unsure for a moment, she looks out of the room to see if her father has returned. Something overwhelms* GRETCHEN *and she collapses back.* MAGGIE *moves to her and pulls the blanket from the bench and across her shoulders. As* GRETCHEN *sobs,* MAGGIE *awkwardly tries to comfort her.*

Gretchen... shhh it's fine now, Gretchen, you're safe now... the doctor will arrive any minute.

This seems to upset her.

GRETCHEN. No! I'm... just some air... I'm...

She tries to stand but is too weak, MAGGIE *grabs her and steadies her on her feet.*

MAGGIE. You can barely stand, Gretchen, please… please…
you're safe now.

GRETCHEN *slumps into* MAGGIE*'s arms. She sobs softly.*

You're safe.

MAGGIE *looks down at the girl in her arms.*

Blackout.

Scene Three

JOSHUA*'s workshop.*

FAN *stands on a table and is wearing an old but beautiful
dress. It is simple, worn.* JOSHUA *awkwardly moves around
her with scissors and a needle and thread, trying to adjust the
dress to fit* FAN *better.* FAN *stands with her arms out, she is in
her element. She speaks as if rehearsing to a large audience.*

FAN. On the last day of the summer, the last day of plenty, I shall
dance. They will call me The Daughter, and they will dress
me in a robe of net and sail, a dress that The Daughters have
worn for a hundred years, and I shall dance. A long long time
ago on the island there was a man, tall and strong, stern yet
kind… and he lived on his own with his daughter near the
harbour. They are The Father and The Daughter. Each day he
would leave her and fish until his boat was full… And this
was all very well for a while until one day the Orca came, all
teeth and foam and her great black dorsal splitting the waves.
At first she was a sight to behold, the children and the women
would crowd the harbour walls if they saw her and the
fishermen would lean long from the sides of their ships
pointing and cheering… soon though, soon the nets began to
be pulled up empty, soon the fish began to look for safer
waters and the sight of the Orca meant empty bellies and light
nets. As winter fast approached The Father looked grim, he
had no food for his daughter and nothing stored for winter.

On the morning of the last day of summer he saw what he must do. Gathering the village at the harbour he reached down and took a length of seaweed and some flowers that had sprouted between the rocks of the harbour wall and he tied them in a crown around The Daughter's head. 'My friends,' he said, 'Tomorrow we shall dance and I shall take my nets out one last time and throw them into the ocean and I will not return until my nets are full.'

JOSHUA. That's good, Fan, you tell it well.

FAN. I don't go on? Maggie says I go on.

JOSHUA. It's just right, tell it just so.

FAN. Has Gretchen woke yet?

JOSHUA. Not yet, I've checked in on her but she's still sleeping, mouth open, snoring like a saw on wood.

FAN. Will she be okay?

JOSHUA. I think so, hard to say with her sending the doctor away like that.

FAN. Why do you think she did that?

JOSHUA. If there's one thing I've learned living with your sister and you, it's that I can ask a thousand question and read a thousand books and I'll still never come close to understanding the workings of a young girl's brain, and it's no easier as they grow older.

FAN. But you don't read any books.

JOSHUA. No, Fan.

FAN. Am I taller than Maggie was, Da? Do you think I'm taller? Maggie says I'm not nearly as pretty as she was... Do you think I'm pretty?

JOSHUA. You know I do.

FAN. As pretty as Maggie was?

JOSHUA (*laughs*). You're as pretty as Maggie was, aye, Fan.

FAN. As pretty as Mother was?

JOSHUA (*beat*). Aye.

FAN. And the dress, you can make it fit?

JOSHUA. Don't get your hopes up, my stitching isn't up to much! I don't need another daughter as miserable as storm clouds stomping around my home. There's only so much I can do. (*Beat.*) And if you're not chosen, I don't think... the village don't look on us too kindly... not with Maggie –

FAN. I shan't be upset, I want to make you proud, for all of us.

JOSHUA. How so?

FAN. For you, for Maggie... if they could see she's not bad, if they can see we're good people, you don't think she's bad, do you?

JOSHUA. Can we just work on the dress, my big fat fingers aren't made for it, they've been stuck with the needle enough times already, if we're to be done by tonight.

FAN. Alright.

There is silence for a moment as JOSHUA *struggles with the dress.*

JOSHUA. I don't think she's bad, Fan... I don't know what to... I don't think she's bad.

FAN. She isn't bad... not bad... she misses Ma like both of us... She told me she loves you.

JOSHUA. Did she now, after that carry on this morning?

FAN. Yesterday, she said... she said that I can steady you, help you with your anger, because you see my mother in me. She said that you'll always be cross at her, that you'll always assume the worst of her... cos you see yourself in her, and that she didn't hate you.

JOSHUA. I don't think that's the same thing.

FAN. Sorry... sorry, Da, it's just... Maybe if I asked her to come, to watch me dance... I don't want...

She trails off.

JOSHUA. Don't want what?

FAN. There's another pile of bread, the baker keeps it in the corner of the shop next to the flour bags. It's all the bits that are a little burnt or old, not bad, just not the best... and they whisper, I didn't notice before... I'd just like to be given the bread from the shelf.

JOSHUA. Fan –

FAN. I'd just like them to smile when they see us and not hear them whisper as we walk away.

JOSHUA stops sewing, he is stuck for words for a moment, he musters a smile.

JOSHUA. It's not so bad here, is it, I'll speak to the baker if... (*Beat.*) I don't think the village will change now, they're stubborn. I think we have to get used to living on the edges.

FAN. But if Maggie came to the party, if she came when I send the ships round the island, if she smiled and danced like she used to and... maybe they would be less angry with her? I don't think she means to lie, to tell lies and to... she's not bad... If she said sorry.

JOSHUA. I'm not sure they are angry, they're... it's like... Anyhow, the less we think on that the better. This is a happy time now, you can wear the dress your sister wore and we'll pick up that pretty garland of flowers that cost me more than I make in a month and you can dance yourself at the party. You'll look like a water sprite.

FAN. D'you think so?

JOSHUA. If I can ever get this dress sorted.

There is silence again whilst FAN thinks and JOSHUA tries to stitch.

FAN. Would you ever leave the village?

JOSHUA. No, I... why do you ask that... no, I don't think so. I grew up here. Me and your ma we, all my life has been here. Why do you ask?

FAN. I was reading, yesterday I was reading one of Maggie's books, and it talked about a palm tree and I thought, if I never live anywhere but here, if I never go anywhere else then I'll never see a palm tree. I'll never, all the things in the books, I'd never see them. I felt sad about that. I love it here, I love our village but... I don't know.

JOSHUA. You're young, Fan, your mind will reach out to far off places, because you think that they're better or more beautiful. Your mother thought about things like that once, like palm trees. You learn as you grow that palm trees are just trees to some folk. The ocean is still the ocean no matter the shade of blue. If you can't find happiness in a place like this you won't find it elsewhere. That's something your sister could learn, there's no better place than another, just different, just changed. If you find a place that lets you stay, once they know who you are... That's the best you'll get... Well, I think that's about the best I'll get this without ripping it up and starting again, get your rough clothes on for now, we need to keep it clean for the dance.

FAN. It's beautiful!

She spins excitedly.

JOSHUA. I'm glad you think so.

FAN *pulls the dress over her head and places it reverently over a nearby chair. She pulls on a shift over her slip.* GRETCHEN *enters from upstairs, she seems unsure on her legs and weakened by her ordeal.*

Well, look who's reached the land of the living... you look pale, girl, are you sure you won't sleep some more?

GRETCHEN. No I'm, I feel lots better, thank you.

JOSHUA. Well, that's good, that's... do you need water? Some food?

GRETCHEN. Water, maybe.

JOSHUA. Fan.

FAN. Would you like it in a cup or a bowl? I sometimes like it in a bowl so I can drink like a cat and –

JOSHUA. Don't confuse the poor girl, just water in a cup.

GRETCHEN. A cup is fine. (*Beat.*) I think I might walk back home after, if it's all the same. I'm feeling stronger now and –

JOSHUA. Oh, not… you don't need to just yet. We've sent word to your mother, someone will be along to collect you shortly, you can't walk the island on your own, not when… not after all you've been through.

GRETCHEN *looks a little worried but is obviously still weak.* FAN *has brought her a cup of water and she drinks.*

GRETCHEN. Oh I, I don't want to be a burden to –

JOSHUA. You're no burden.

GRETCHEN. All the same, I'm sure I can walk.

JOSHUA. There'll be someone along shortly.

GRETCHEN. But –

JOSHUA. I'm sorry, Gretchen, I have to… for your own good, I'm going to have to insist. You're no trouble here, we're happy to have you until then, and what with the doctor not taking a look over you I'd not live with myself if you didn't make it home, please… just rest for a while longer and soon you can get back to your own bed. Do the clothes fit okay?

GRETCHEN. Oh yes, they're just fine, thank you.

FAN. You look beautiful in Maggie's dress, she doesn't wear that any more, she doesn't like the flowers. You can probably keep it, can't she, Da?

JOSHUA. I'm sure she won't want it back.

FAN. See, you look very pretty in it.

GRETCHEN. Thank you. Where's Maggie now?

JOSHUA. She's gutting fish for supper, round back.

FAN. I can't stand the guts.

Beat.

JOSHUA. Well, shall we walk into town and pick up that crown of yours, Fan?

FAN. Yes please!

JOSHUA. Alright, girl, come along, rest up here, Gretchen, it won't be long and someone will collect you. Promise me you won't try anything foolish, you'll stay put?

GRETCHEN *finishes her water.*

GRETCHEN. Yes, I will, thank you.

JOSHUA. Good… good, well, we'll be back shortly, Maggie is just out back should you need anything.

GRETCHEN. Thank you.

JOSHUA *and* FAN *leave the room,* FAN *is a ball of excitement.* GRETCHEN *watches them go for a moment. She walks to* FAN*'s dress and picks it up, studying it. Slowly she unfolds it and holds it to her cheek, feeling the fabric against her skin.*

She closes her eyes. After a moment she places the dress back as she found it and walks to the workbench. She picks up the scissors, staring at the blades, still looking at the dress.

MAGGIE *enters, hands bloodied with a bucket and a knife in her hands. She does not see* GRETCHEN. GRETCHEN *replaces the scissors quickly, unnoticed by* MAGGIE. *Suddenly* GRETCHEN *speaks.*

Does it not make you sick?

MAGGIE *starts and turns to look at her, her hands bloodied.*

MAGGIE. God, Gretchen, don't make me jump like that.

GRETCHEN *rests weakly on a chair.*

GRETCHEN. I'm sorry... It doesn't make you... all the blood and... their eyes?

MAGGIE. I don't mind it so.

GRETCHEN. I wanted to thank you, for helping me.

MAGGIE. There's no need, I did nothing but sit, the fishermen pulled you out of the water.

GRETCHEN. I know... Still.

MAGGIE *looks up at her for a moment. She takes the gratitude and smiles.*

MAGGIE. It's a pleasure, are you feeling better now?

GRETCHEN. Yes, I feel good but weak, better though. I've slept upstairs, I've been asleep.

MAGGIE. I didn't think I'd see you up and about so swiftly.

GRETCHEN. Yes, just a drink, I needed a drink.

MAGGIE. Good. That dress suits you, you look pretty.

GRETCHEN. Thank you, your da said, thank you. Well, I'll leave you if you like, if you're busy...

MAGGIE (*beat*). You should still see the doctor, Da said you asked to send him away.

GRETCHEN. Oh, yes, I'm fine now so... just a drink and some rest.

MAGGIE. There could be something inside you, something we can't see, that could hurt you.

GRETCHEN. I'm... I feel fine now so...

MAGGIE *can see she doesn't want to be pressed.*

MAGGIE. Anyway, it's none of mine, just safer, that's all.

GRETCHEN. Maybe I will, later, after I've gone home.

MAGGIE. If you feel better then I'm going to get back to the supper.

GRETCHEN. Yes, yes I should, I'll go back up and wait. (*Beat*.) Have you been to the mainland, to any of the other islands?

MAGGIE. No not... no. I've been to the market with Da to sell his things, but not any further. It's a day's sail away, mainland is even further, we don't go out on the ocean much. Why?

GRETCHEN. I wondered, I remembered when you were The Daughter, when you told the story, you didn't tell it like normal, you talked about other things... birds and animals that we don't have here, and the voices, you did the different voices, I thought you must have.

MAGGIE. I got in quite a bit of trouble for that from Da, he told me the appearance of a giraffe in the village story did nothing for it but make a mockery of the whole thing.

GRETCHEN (*laughs*). I liked it.

MAGGIE. My mother was from the mainland, but I've never visited, only read about it, seen pictures.

GRETCHEN. What's it like?

MAGGIE. It's, well, there's so much of it, it's hard to know where to start, some is like here, like us, some is... different, bigger, too big, Ma said, she came to the market with her da, to buy fish, sell nets. That's where she met my da, and then she married him, and she came here. She said she liked living in a place where you knew each person by name. Said the mainland was too cold, too big.

GRETCHEN. That's nice.

MAGGIE. It's horse shit is what it is. She hated it here, hated the people, hated their tiny minds. She stayed for my da, because she loved him. (*Beat*.) What were you doing out there? On your own? It's dangerous, boats drift into the spill, the currents are strong, you can end up strung out over the rock.

GRETCHEN. I was lucky. I won't, I won't go out again. Your sister, she looks at me like... It was like she's never seen me before.

MAGGIE *laughs*.

MAGGIE. That's cos she thinks you're a mermaid.

GRETCHEN *looks confused.*

She thinks that's how they pulled you from the sea, that you're from some underwater city where they all have fishtails for legs, it doesn't matter. Have you heard from your mother yet?

GRETCHEN. Not yet, she'll come… She really thinks I'm a mermaid?

MAGGIE. My sister is a funny fish, Gretchen, she's smarter than the rest of the island put together but there are some things she clings to. She's certain there are fairies and goblins, she's terrified that the Orca's wrath will lay waste to us all, and she so desperately wants there to be mermaids that she runs laps around the harbour every time a dolphin breaks the water.

GRETCHEN*'s nerves leave her for a moment and she cracks a smile briefly.* MAGGIE *smiles in return.*

She thinks you've given up your tail to come ashore and find the man you love.

GRETCHEN. Well, I think I like that better than the truth. Maybe I shan't put her straight just yet. (*Beat.*) It's your sister's turn to dance? I saw her dress. She wants to be picked, to be The Daughter?

MAGGIE. That's right.

There is a pregnant silence between them. GRETCHEN *watches for* MAGGIE*'s reaction when she finally speaks.*

Were you heading out or heading in?

GRETCHEN. What?

MAGGIE. When… the boat, when you fell… did you fall?

GRETCHEN. Yes… I was out, on the way out…

MAGGIE. And were you fishing?

Beat.

GRETCHEN. I think… it's not good for me I don't think, trying to remember what…

MAGGIE *can see she is getting flustered, she backs off.*

MAGGIE. That's alright, I don't, you don't need to tell me.

GRETCHEN. It's not… it was a blur really, it's not that I don't want to tell you, I don't remember much… I saw the Orca pod, she was in the waves with her calves and the next thing I knew… It was huge, the ocean… huge and heavy and…

MAGGIE. The Orca?

GRETCHEN. Yes, the pod in the –

MAGGIE. Were you scared?

GRETCHEN. I… no, not of her, no.

MAGGIE. Me neither. I've seen her too.

GRETCHEN. Really?

MAGGIE. When I was The Daughter, she came up to the boat as they pulled me aboard. The men were screaming, thrashing, shouting for their spears as if the sky was falling, she stayed calm, still.

GRETCHEN. When my da… the men said they'd seen her off the spill, red teeth, waiting, sent a party to hunt her.

MAGGIE. Stupid…

GRETCHEN. What?

MAGGIE. Such hate, it's stupid…

GRETCHEN. She scares the catch, she's a curse, bad luck.

MAGGIE. So they say.

GRETCHEN. Was for me…

MAGGIE. Maybe, but you didn't drown, did you?

GRETCHEN *half-smiles.*

GRETCHEN. No.

MAGGIE. And you can return home whenever you want now…
when you're well.

The smile fades a little more. MAGGIE *notices.*

GRETCHEN. Yes.

MAGGIE. You went out too, after me, you were chosen.

GRETCHEN (*beat*). Yes.

Neither speaks for a moment.

MAGGIE. There's a dog, big dog, at Frank Travellion's house,
one of the dock workers. The dog is huge and clever, for a
dog, it does a lot… Not just tricks and stuff but useful things.
It goes out in the morning and brings in the milk, they leave
it in a special box with a handle he can grab in his jaws and
he brings it in for Frank. Frank's leg got all mangled in an
accident on one of the boats, got caught in a rope, and he
can't walk properly. He has a crutch now and the dog helps
him… and I think this has made him sad because he drinks
lots now, he doesn't have a wife, she died and he's ugly so…
He drinks and he hits the dog, really hits it. I tried to stop
him once. I shouted for him to stop. But Frank just looked at
me like I'd told him the moon was square, he just said 'It's a
dog' like… as if it didn't matter. I thought then… I looked at
the dog and I thought, you've got teeth… you've got… use
them, tear the bastard apart… or if not, run away with the
milk or, but he doesn't, he gets the milk, he takes the
beatings and he wags his tail and smiles every time Frank
throws him a treat… 'It's a dog.'

She looks at GRETCHEN, *unsure if she's comprehended.*

If you don't want to go home, don't.

GRETCHEN *looks suddenly more uncomfortable.*

I think I'll carry on now if it's all the same to you, I really do
have a lot to do today.

MAGGIE *stands to leave and takes a few steps…*

GRETCHEN. You shouldn't let her go.

MAGGIE *looks up to* GRETCHEN, *meeting her eyes.* GRETCHEN *looks away and pulls her blanket in close around.*

I think I should like to be a mermaid. I think I'll go back to bed until I'm collected, would you mind? I'm so very tired.

MAGGIE. Of course, I'll fetch you when they arrive... of course.

GRETCHEN *turns and walks back upstairs.* MAGGIE *continues to prepare lunch.*

FAN *tells her story for the dance as she did with* JOSHUA. *It is another place, not in the house, away from this time and location.* MAGGIE *continues to prepare dinner, unaware, whilst* FAN *speaks.*

FAN. When day came, The Daughter woke to find a dress hanging on the bottom of her bed, stitched from nets and old sails and patches from The Father's cloak and hat. She jumped up from her bed and put it on, it was a perfect fit, and if he had spent a year's wages on any dress from the mainland it shouldn't have looked half as beautiful. The Daughter ran through the village waking the fishermen, and one and all spilled into the square. For the first time in an age there was laughter and dancing, The Daughter spun and jumped and the villagers danced, clapping each other on the back, and soon came the time for The Father to sail. He turned to the villagers and said, 'Light the lamps for me all along the harbour walls as I may not return until the sun is long gone. Light the lamps so I can see my way to port.' He turned and climbed on to the deck of his ship. The village looked out to sea and saw the black fin of the Orca, it cut back and forth, stirring and crashing the waves to white. It leapt and dived and crashed into the sea and the clouds began to gather and the sea began to roar as if to say, 'Come now, come and face me, come and find me, come and fear me.'

MAGGIE *finishes preparing the vegetables.* JOSHUA *enters carrying the garland.* MAGGIE *looks at it, missing a beat, she looks to her father.* JOSHUA's *anger from before is still present but he has calmed, it is more for show.*

MAGGIE. Where's Fan?

JOSHUA. Run off to get ribbon for her shoes. (*Bemused.*) Says she can't dance without it.

MAGGIE. Are you free, Da?

JOSHUA *nods*.

JOSHUA. Make it swift, girl.

MAGGIE *hesitates for a moment, unsure whether to carry on. She decides to speak.*

MAGGIE. I've been trying to remember something that we did with Ma. I wanted to ask you, I remember when all of us were small, when Fan was still a baby, for a holiday once we went to the mainland. I remember getting on the boat, I remember red strawberries, on my dress there were tiny red strawberries... But that didn't happen, did it? We haven't gone out of the islands, we haven't gone to the mainland? It's not clear, my memory, it's blurred, it's... Did we ever go?

JOSHUA *is clearly uncomfortable*.

JOSHUA. I have a thousand things to do today –

MAGGIE *pushes on*.

MAGGIE. I remember the ocean, I remember the boat was huge, but it couldn't have been because I remember hanging my hand from the side in the cool water, I remember how it felt on my hand, cool, and I was scared because I thought the Orca might come and sink us. I remember Fan crying, Mum fed her and said it didn't matter if people saw, saw her feeding her baby like that, because we weren't on the island any more and... she said that on the mainland people didn't mind so much. That there were so many people that people had stopped caring about the affairs of others. I think I remember that you got cross at that, I think you told her to hide herself, but she smiled and you weren't cross any more. I can remember things, I don't think I've made it up.

JOSHUA. That's enough now.

MAGGIE. I just wanted –

JOSHUA. Well, don't, and don't think that I've, I've not forgotten... this morning!

MAGGIE. Why don't you speak about her?

JOSHUA. Maggie!

MAGGIE. Sorry.

JOSHUA looks at MAGGIE, her apology stops him. It doesn't happen often. He softens for a moment and remembers.

JOSHUA. We never went to the mainland, it was your mother. Mr Simmonds used to hire the little sailboats, your mother hired the biggest one he had, one that would fit us all in, and we sailed from the dockyard all the way round to the other side of the island, past the harbour to the other end of the beach. We hadn't got much money, we couldn't really go anywhere. Your mother had moved all the furniture in the house around. Told you it was an inn, that we were on the mainland... You remember that?

MAGGIE. I do, I did, I thought it, that it couldn't have been real.

JOSHUA. It was, sort of.

MAGGIE. Thank you.

Beat.

JOSHUA. I don't, it's not that I don't want to remember... Enough of that now.

MAGGIE. I'm sorry, Da.

JOSHUA. And which one on the list should I fix that 'sorry' to?

MAGGIE. Whatever you like.

MAGGIE walks to him and hugs him. He freezes, confused.

JOSHUA. Did you need something, girl?

MAGGIE. In a moment, not yet, this first.

JOSHUA holds his daughter; for a moment they are still.

That's what else I remember. Your arms, safe.

This is becoming uncomfortable for JOSHUA.

JOSHUA. Is everything alright, has something, did something happen?

Suddenly THE FATHER *enters. He is huge, a bear of a man. His older years do not diminish him at all. He is rugged and strong. There is a tension between them.* JOSHUA *will not look him in the eye and awkwardly shuffles his feet.* MAGGIE *jumps back.* THE FATHER *sees her and there is a moment, brief and unspoken, but something passes between them.*

MAGGIE. Da?

THE FATHER. Ah Joshua, how are you this morning, getting ready for the dance no doubt?

JOSHUA. Father! What can we... Christ, it's a mess here, Father, if I'd known... Maggie, will you fetch some cider, would you like a drink, Father? Something to –

THE FATHER. Not for me, thank you. I'm here for Gretchen, I didn't want the young thing injuring herself further, not on today of all days... and business, business is good, Joshua?

JOSHUA. If we'd known... As good as ever, the houses, the ships... there's much work here for a carpenter.

THE FATHER. Important work! The village couldn't survive without the work you do, remember that, Joshua.

JOSHUA. Yes... thank you.

THE FATHER. And how is your little Fan? I hear from all across the village she is quite the character.

JOSHUA. I can barely hold her still for excitement, Father, she can't wait for the evening to come.

THE FATHER. Of course... of course! Well, down to business.

JOSHUA. Yes, Father. Go fetch Gretchen, Maggie, she's upstairs, Father, been resting up there in Fan's room.

MAGGIE. Da...

JOSHUA (*harder*). Will you do as you're told, girl, don't keep
  The Father waiting.

MAGGIE. Da, can I speak with you a moment in –

THE FATHER. It's alright, Joshua. Since I'm here, I wondered
  if I might speak with you, with both of you, Maggie?

He looks at her kindly, imploring.

Please sit.

JOSHUA *does so,* MAGGIE *hesitates.*

Please.

MAGGIE. I have chores –

THE FATHER. You can do your chores when I'm finished.
  That's right, isn't it, Joshua, just listen now and I think you'll
  feel a whole lot better when I'm done. Today, whatever you
  may think of it, this day to the people here – it's everything.
  We have done this for as long as anyone can remember, The
  Father before me and the one before that, for as long as is
  written at the very least. It's not just something we do,
  Maggie, it's something we are... Do you understand? It's
  something that's a part of us, woven into the netting,
  hammered into the hulls, if you'll allow me some poetry...
  and to miss it, to ignore it. To throw it away like it were
  something dirty and useless... Do you understand, girl? This
  village isn't big enough that a girl missing at the dance isn't
  noticed, and it's enough. It's enough, you could pull it all
  apart, this thing that we do, the dance, The Daughter's
  boat... all of it, because whatever you believe it will take its
  toll... It might not be the Orca that stays the fish but if the
  village don't get what they want, if a crack begins to form,
  you can be sure things will start to spoil. We're only as
  strong as the weakest of us. One girl, against the happiness
  of the whole village... Can you not see it has to be done?

He pauses and mops his brow for a moment.

Would you fetch me that drink, Joshua, I fear the heat may
be taking its toll a little after all.

JOSHUA. Of course, Father.

Beat.

THE FATHER. Now, to these accusations, these foul lies. A great
hurt you did to me, that you could level such hate at me after
the things I've done for you here, the work I've sent your
family. I know how you were hurting when your mother
passed. I know how the village have treated you, I know they
haven't always done right by you, by her. God knows we
didn't see eye to eye, we didn't agree on anything much at all,
and I know that maybe I could have said more, to help, with
the village...

He takes a long drink and mops his brow again.

And I want to apologise.

MAGGIE *looks to* JOSHUA.

I want to apologise and I want to offer you something in the
way of recompense.

JOSHUA. There's really no need to –

THE FATHER. Do you think you could see your way to
forgiving us all?

MAGGIE *doesn't move.*

If you could understand what your lies could do. The lies of
one, angry, lonely and hurt little girl... a little girl who
desperately misses her mother, a child who is angry at the
village that shunned her.

MAGGIE *begins to well up, her jaw sets, but she remains
silent.*

I know how you must have felt, girl, this village is a cold and
quarterless place for those on the outside, and your mother...
well, she put herself on the outside as often as not.

MAGGIE. My mother –

THE FATHER. Your mother was a wonderful woman and
deserved better than she got, but to pull this place apart, to

sink it out of... of hatred and rage, girl... No more lies or troublemaking, Maggie. If you can promise me this, well, I think the village may just surprise you. Stubborn they may be but they have a large heart between them, I think they will forgive and forget... And to show them, to turn a new page so to speak, I'd like to escort you and your family to the dance this evening... What do you say, Joshua, you can walk to the dance at my side with your daughters, proud... no more whispers, no more talk behind your back... no more scowls, Maggie, no more feeling like you don't belong. And this island can be whole again. Then this island, this village, will become a happier and a safer place. I guarantee it... Come to the dance, see for yourself.

MAGGIE *is silent*.

JOSHUA. Will you just tell him... no more... please... will you tell him that and go and fetch Gretchen and we can go back to... we can start over, Maggie.

THE FATHER. It's okay, Joshua, don't push the girl, it must be difficult, but think of Fan.

The hairs on MAGGIE*'s neck stand on end at the mention of her sister.*

JOSHUA. We need to move on, Maggie.

MAGGIE *looks to* JOSHUA *pleadingly*.

MAGGIE. Da...

THE FATHER. Yours was a special one, Maggie, did she tell you, Joshua?

JOSHUA *shrugs*.

As we held her over the side, the pod appeared, only happened once before, the pod appeared and she looked straight at you. Didn't she, girl? Just like in the story. A special one it was.

JOSHUA. You didn't tell me that, is that true?

MAGGIE. That's right...

THE FATHER *continues in a jolly tone, laughing to himself and talking like they are old friends.*

THE FATHER. It's true, as I live and breathe, swam up to the boat and looked her straight in the eyes as we pulled her aboard. She didn't cry or scream or...

MAGGIE. No, I wasn't, I was cold and... I wasn't scared.

JOSHUA. How did she look?

MAGGIE. I don't recall much, I was cold...

THE FATHER. We were out a long time with you, Maggie, as I remember...

MAGGIE. My wrists...

THE FATHER. Trouble with pulling you aboard. It's not pleasant sometimes, the ocean, what she does. I know that, I've been making my living from her my whole life, but to this village she is everything. Mother, wife and daughter. Your father understands that, your sister too. If you take away something that's been there beneath us all for so long you cause chaos, there's nothing there and people feel unsafe and they feel lost and it all comes tumbling down on our heads. You can't fight the tide, Maggie... there are too many in this village that need this, need this not to be tossed aside. You can't fight the tide, Maggie. Do you understand, girl?

MAGGIE. I understand.

THE FATHER. Can I count on you to do what's right, by your family, by the village?

MAGGIE. What's right?

THE FATHER. Will you come to the dance, will you stop this nonsense, will you come to watch the girls dance this afternoon.

MAGGIE. Da... Please.

THE FATHER *glances at* JOSHUA *who withers under his stare.*

JOSHUA. Listen to him, girl, for all our sakes.

MAGGIE *looks to* THE FATHER.

MAGGIE. I'll come.

THE FATHER. Well, there it is, that wasn't so hard?

JOSHUA. Thank you, Father.

THE FATHER. Well then, if you could just fetch Gretchen, I'll be going, lots to do. (*Beat.*) This is a good thing, Maggie, a change for you, it takes a big thing to make a big change. Come and dance with your village, laugh with us. If we can get through today then... I think you could find your way back to us, back to the life you had before. You want that, don't you? For things to be better for yourself, for your family... for Fan?

MAGGIE. For Fan, yes, Father.

THE FATHER *stands and shakes* JOSHUA's *hand.*

THE FATHER. Good... Good... Dear little Fan.

MAGGIE's *eyes are burning furiously.* GRETCHEN *enters and stops aghast.* THE FATHER *stiffens, suddenly tense. Everyone is aware of the tension and no one speaks for a moment.* GRETCHEN *is white as a sheet, petrified.*

Well, Gretchen... Are you well? Gave us all a scare you did, on this day of all days too, you could have died!

GRETCHEN *doesn't answer.* JOSHUA *speaks, trying to break the mood.*

JOSHUA. She's been recovering quicker than any of us could have thought. We've been caring for her, haven't we, girl.

GRETCHEN *nods, unable to speak.* THE FATHER *looks from* GRETCHEN *to* MAGGIE *and back. For a moment the softness in his voice disappears, replaced with thinly veiled contempt.*

THE FATHER. Quite the flock of geese.

JOSHUA. You're looking much better. (*Jovially.*) I thought this morning that it'd be days, if not longer, before –

THE FATHER. So they fished you out of the sea, was it, salted, wet and shaking no doubt. You were lucky, girl, most of the fleet off, lucky, a lucky escape. I shall get you safely home, Gretchen, today of all days. Come on, girl, there's lots to be done.

GRETCHEN *looks terrified at* MAGGIE.

MAGGIE. She's going to stay a while, Father, if it's all the same, she has my dress on and I'll need it for later, I said I'd help her with her braids and all for the dance too.

JOSHUA. Maggie!

THE FATHER. She won't be going to the dance, Maggie, not after today... could have died.

MAGGIE. I shall walk her home then, Father, you're busy and –

THE FATHER. Not too busy to look after one of our own.

The threat is clear but not overstated.

Beat.

MAGGIE. Shall I walk with you, Gretchen?

THE FATHER *looks to* MAGGIE, *then to* GRETCHEN, *who is terrified.*

THE FATHER. Come along, Gretchen.

GRETCHEN *looks at* MAGGIE, *imploring her to say no more.* THE FATHER *looks at* MAGGIE *warily.*

He turns to leave and GRETCHEN *follows, she looks at* MAGGIE *as she passes.*

JOSHUA. Maggie, why must you bait him so, an olive branch he offers us, a chance for you, for Fan! He's not the devil you make him out to be, he's nothing to be fearful of.

MAGGIE. I'm not scared of him, Da.

JOSHUA. Can you not just make peace –

MAGGIE. Da, you need to listen to me now, you need to –

JOSHUA. Cos all this needs to stop, what do you think Fan would feel if she heard what you'd said to the rest of the village about The Father? What do you think that would do to her?

MAGGIE. We need to tell her, we need her to –

JOSHUA. You dare! One word of this filth, these lies, and I swear to you!

MAGGIE. Da, please.

JOSHUA. No, Maggie, no! If your lies reach her ears then... like before, if she hears anything from you, if you tell her anything. My patience with you will end. Christ, girl, will you stop! Will you look at what you're doing to us, scraping a living, eating from the bottom of the pot! The way they look at us here – and it's you.

Beat.

MAGGIE. It's... Da, please... I need to talk to you about Fan, about tonight, about... dancing for The Father.

JOSHUA *stands, angry, and walks away from* MAGGIE.

JOSHUA. For Christ's sake, Maggie –

MAGGIE *snaps.*

MAGGIE. DA! Will you just listen, open your damned ears and listen, you have to listen! Don't let her go. Please, promise me, if she's chosen don't send her out on the boat with them.

JOSHUA. I said to you, Maggie, this has to stop now!

MAGGIE. There's no one else here, just me, and I know... I know there's doubt in your mind, that you're afraid of –

JOSHUA. Maggie! –

MAGGIE. Of what the village might, I don't know what but please –

JOSHUA. Stop it now.

MAGGIE. Listen to me. If she's chosen, if they choose her –

JOSHUA. I'm warning you, girl.

MAGGIE. For Christ's sake, Da, she can't get on that boat, if Ma could see you now, like this, scared to –

JOSHUA hits her hard, too hard. She hits the floor, and for a moment doesn't move.

JOSHUA. Nothing but hurt, your lies have brought nothing but... You do your damnedest to pull us all apart... they're good men, the men you... good men... Get up!

She begins to stir. MAGGIE pulls herself on to a chair.

What do you think their wives would have thought, their daughters and sons? They risk their lives every day out on the water and for what thanks, to be accused of all sorts of sordid, evil...

MAGGIE shakily stands, brushing herself off.

Not a word to Fan, you hear? Not a... or I'm done with you.

MAGGIE. You're a coward, Joshua Finn, you're no father, no husband, my mother would spit on you if she could see you now.

JOSHUA. Don't talk about my wife –

MAGGIE. You're a coward!

JOSHUA turns and walks from the house. Eventually MAGGIE pulls herself to, nursing her face. She moves to the table, unsure what to do with herself. She shakily picks up the knife and attempts to cut some of the vegetables again but it is too much, she begins to sob gently.

Suddenly FAN arrives home, huffing and puffing and carrying her flower crown. FAN launches into her speech, she doesn't notice MAGGIE's face at first.

FAN. The Orca! The Devil smiled and marvelled this, 'How loud, how vile silence is.' It's the Orca, your riddle.

MAGGIE *tries to pull herself together.*

MAGGIE. You can sit for a moment before you go answering riddles if you like... Did you see Da?

FAN. Not since before. It's the Orca, they're silent in the water, that's how they sneak up on you, are you not impressed?

MAGGIE. It's not the Orca.

FAN. Of course it is, what else is there bad? There's foxes but they're small and they aren't that frightening and –

MAGGIE. It's not the Orca... You don't have to be bad to do wrong, for it to happen. Maybe have another go, and think of it yourself, don't go to Da or anyone else in the village because they couldn't think their way out of a fishing net!

FAN *catches the tone of rebuke and shrinks a little.*

FAN. Alright... are you cross with me?

MAGGIE. No, I'm... (*Beat.*) Listen to me for a moment, I need to ask you something, about the dance.

FAN. I'm not sure I can talk, Maggie, when I think about it my belly wriggles and jiggles like it's full of eels and I feel like I might pop. I was thinking, it's like the great parties in the storybooks, it's like our village has its very own one of those. Tara Spinney met her husband at the dance, she said they danced all night and it was magical.

FAN *can sense suddenly that something is wrong.*

What's the matter? You look all white...

She sees the blood on MAGGIE*'s cheek from her nose, her red cheek.* MAGGIE *stops trying to hide it.*

Oh God, Maggie! What happened? Are you...

She stops in her tracks. Beat.

Did Da...?

MAGGIE. It's fine, it doesn't hurt it's –

FAN. Da hit you?

MAGGIE. Yes... he did, yes but I'm fine, it's not –

FAN. What have you done?

Beat.

MAGGIE. What?

FAN. Oh, not today please, you can't fight today, you can't
wind him up or argue or... Please, whatever you've done,
not today, Maggie, please... for me, for today, please!

MAGGIE. I haven't –

FAN. Please...

MAGGIE. No, it's not... I haven't done a thing!

FAN. Whatever it is, whatever you've done to make him hit
you. It's my day, my chance to... I don't want it spoiled.

MAGGIE. What I've done! Our bastard of a da –

FAN. I don't think you should say things like that about Da, he
loves you, he said as much this morning.

MAGGIE. He did, did he?

FAN. As close as, he said he didn't think you were bad.

MAGGIE. That's not the same thing. (*Beat.*) Please, I can't...
I need to talk with you.

FAN. Well, I want to ask you something as well. (*Beat.*) I want
you to come, to the dance, I want you to be there. I think
even if I wasn't chosen, if you were there, if you could come,
that might be magical too –

MAGGIE. I'm not coming, you promised you'd never ask.

FAN. But I think if you did, I think it might all start to change.
If you could just come for an hour, for half an hour even and
dance and smile like you used to. Please think about it, the
people in the village are –

MAGGIE. There are no people, the village isn't people, it's one
cruel person. When they come together they are one tall thug
of a man and they're deaf and dumb and mute to anything

that frightens them. I won't spend another minute surrounded by their looks and their whispers, do you hear? You can't ask that of me, you shouldn't!

FAN. I'm sorry but –

MAGGIE. Don't be sorry, be angry, be… I don't know, be something other than these people, they're poison.

FAN. Maggie!

MAGGIE. They are, and they'll swallow you whole.

Beat.

FAN. It's you.

MAGGIE. What?

FAN. It's you, it's your fault, they don't hate me, they didn't hate Ma and they don't hate Da either. It's you! Your lies, and your mischief and all the nonsense you've been –

MAGGIE. Christ, you're a child. You have to grow up fast, you have to start thinking for yourself. You're not ten any more.

FAN. You shouldn't swear so much, I know, I know I don't want to be a child, I don't want to be, I want to be strong like… I want to be brave… to be something the village look up to like Ma.

MAGGIE. The village didn't look up to our ma, they smiled at her and laughed with her at her jokes and behind closed doors they laughed at her, at her reading, at her strange ways. Do you not remember, they tore at her and they broke her until –

FAN. She drowned. They loved her.

MAGGIE. Ask Da why she drowned, ask Da why she was out there.

FAN. No! (*Beat.*) No! What are you saying!

MAGGIE. Remember, Fan, try to –

FAN. You're lying! Why are you always lying? Please, stop this, come tonight, we could dance… even if they do stare, even if they don't talk to us, please come and dance with me, come and... and help them remember, what you were like before, before Mother and –

MAGGIE. Fan, I –

FAN. Help me remember... please.

MAGGIE. I need you not to dance, little Fan.

There is a long silence as FAN *looks at the floor.*

FAN. Da thinks you're broken.

MAGGIE. I'm not... This isn't about me, this is –

FAN. He thinks you'll not stop until you pull the village down with you.

MAGGIE. Listen, when I was The Daughter, when I wore the dress and told the tale, something happened. Something foul and... something... and I told Da, and he told me to do nothing so I told the village and they told me it was nothing and now I'm frightened. It's not that nobody believed me, Fan, it's that they won't, they won't believe me... they can't or... and now I'm scared... I'm scared because I think the same has happened... to others, to Gretchen and maybe to you if you went, if you were to... Please...

Beat.

FAN. I want you to come to the dance.

MAGGIE. FAN! Please listen, The Father –

FAN. If you came maybe, if you –

MAGGIE. Fan, you remember... when I came ashore, you remember.

FAN. The village might –

MAGGIE. My skirt was ripped.

FAN. Stop lying –

MAGGIE. There was blood on –

FAN. Please stop lying –

MAGGIE. Please –

FAN. You're lying, Maggie.

Beat.

MAGGIE. Fan, please… not you!

Beat.

FAN. I'm going to put on my dress and my garland and I'm going to dance, I want you to be there, I do.

MAGGIE *stares at* FAN, *she realises she won't believe her. She walks from the house and* FAN *is sat alone.*

Blackout.

Scene Four

FAN *alone on stage.*

FAN *practises her story as she did with* JOSHUA.

FAN. No sooner had The Father reached the open ocean than a great storm whipped up the waves into a fury. The Orca raged and crashed herself against The Father's boat, every time The Father tried to toss his nets into the ocean, the Orca's sharp jaws would snap at him and tear at the ropes. All through the day, stood tall in the eye of the storm, The Father fought with the Orca, barely keeping his boat afloat. He began to tire, his hands wet, cold and raw, his legs burning and stiff, all seemed lost… Suddenly, crisp and clear he heard the harbour bells ring out across the waves, echoing within the storm. The Father looked back across the waves to see the lamps burning bright on the sea wall, when suddenly something caught his eye. In the gloom he saw a tiny rowboat picking its way across the white water. As it got closer and closer to him he saw The Daughter, stood in her net dress and her flower crown, being tossed and thrown by the waves in her beautiful sea-blue boat. He waved to her, he shouted and screamed for her to return but his cries were lost in the winds and rain. When she wasn't but a few feet from him the Orca turned, seeing her approach. The Father cried for her to turn to flee but at that moment, as the Orca sank beneath the waves to start her attack, as The Father shouted himself hoarse, The Daughter stood and smiled… she smiled and as the great white teeth broke the surface she leapt… She leapt into her open jaws.

Scene Five

JOSHUA*'s workshop.*

JOSHUA *is stood at the door looking nervously out. He is dressed smartly, as smartly as he can muster, in an old suit. He checks his watch,* FAN *enters down the stairs, dressed in the dress that* JOSHUA *had been working on.*

JOSHUA. You look a picture, little Fan. And not a moment too soon, The Father will be here any minute.

FAN. What time is it?

JOSHUA. Almost nine-thirty.

FAN. It feels later. The sky looks later. I've been looking from the window for Maggie. (*Beat.*) Da, I don't think… I don't know if she'll come…

JOSHUA. She has a minute or so, give her a minute.

Beat.

FAN. But if she doesn't.

JOSHUA. Give her a minute… Please.

FAN. Sorry, Da.

JOSHUA *ventures a smile.*

JOSHUA. She promised The Father, she may yet surprise us both. There's still time. She must see, what this means, what this could be for us all, to walk beside The Father. Whatever else she's my daughter, your sister, she must understand what this could mean.

Beat.

FAN. We had a fight, she told me… she said some things…

JOSHUA. What… she… what did she tell you?

FAN. I don't think she'll come.

JOSHUA looks panicked.

JOSHUA. What did she say?!

As he is speaking THE FATHER *enters.* THE FATHER *seems on edge, tense.*

THE FATHER. Ahh, just the girl. My goodness, you look every bit The Daughter, doesn't she.

JOSHUA. Good evening, Father, that she does.

THE FATHER. All the beauty of your sister.

FAN. Thank you, Father.

JOSHUA. Aye, and none of the frowns. You're a sea sprite, aren't you, girl!

THE FATHER. That she is, and are you ready to dance?

FAN. I am. Da has fixed up Mother's dress and I have practised the story too.

THE FATHER. And I'm sure you tell it well.

FAN. I will! If I'm picked I mean.

Beat.

THE FATHER. And you'd like that, to be picked?

FAN looks to JOSHUA, who nods in approval.

FAN. Yes I… I would yes.

THE FATHER. Well, you are a dear thing, aren't you. We shall see, shan't we, little miss… Come on then, girl, the tides soon won't be with us, we need to be away. The black water calls. Where's the girl, Joshua, where's Maggie?

JOSHUA. I… we're coming down to the harbour for the dance, Fan is… I expect Maggie will meet us there or –

THE FATHER. Is she not here?

JOSHUA. Not yet, Father, I'm sure she's –

THE FATHER. That won't do, not at all, if she's not here, it must be now, Joshua, it must be all of you. Anything else and…

JOSHUA. Fan just spoke with her, what did you say to her, Fan?

FAN. I told her to come, I wanted her to –

JOSHUA. See, I expect she'll be coming along soon, any –

THE FATHER *is visibly agitated.*

THE FATHER. If she's not here, if she won't walk with us… I won't sugarcoat it, it's her defiance, her lies that have put your family here. I'm sorry, I truly am but no more. Chance after chance she's thrown back at us.

JOSHUA. I could, should I look for her, Father?

THE FATHER. There's no time, no time to be running across an island to find your black sheep.

JOSHUA. Surely… there must be a way, for Fan, Father, this day means so much to her. She's been looking forward to it since she can remember.

THE FATHER. And the other girls in the village, have they not? I'm sorry, Fan, I truly am, there comes a time when I have to think about the village, the community. I've given her chance after chance. (*Beat.*) You need to know a thing when it's before you, Joshua, a bad apple, a chance of redemption.

FAN. She's not bad, Father, she's… she's sad I think, please don't hate her.

THE FATHER. I'm afraid my feelings don't carry as far as you think, it's the village, the island.

FAN. I know she could come back to us, Father, I know it. She loves me, and Da too, she loves us. If she could just see what this means to us, what the village means to us. Please, Father, is there nothing can be done?

Beat.

THE FATHER. Well, you are a marvel, little Fan (*Beat.*) You know there might just be. What do you know of the orcas, Fan?

FAN. I've heard stories, Father, lots of stories.

THE FATHER. They aren't like others in the ocean, girl, there's a dash of something there, behind their eyes. They aren't just a sharp set of teeth and the smell of blood. They're clever enough to know, to know themselves, but that's dangerous you see, that's what gets them, that's the end of them.

FAN. How d'you mean?

THE FATHER. Well, for instance, girl, last spring the men and I had cornered half the pod in the shallows. Two of the young ones and a larger one, a mother I think. We'd boxed them in with the hull of the ships against the cliffs and they had nowhere to run. The little ones were scared, squawking and bleating like lambs in the water as the larger one thrashed and rolled, looking for an escape. We were closing in. (*Beat.*) They were done for, little Fan, when some damn fool who had forgotten to loose his sails catches a breeze and for a moment, for the smallest of minutes, there's a gap.

FAN. And they got out?

THE FATHER. Almost… the mother could've sprung at the gap quick as you like, but not the little ones. Scared or… they didn't move, didn't budge… and the bigger one, she turns and calls but they stay there on the surface. So she turns, she swims back by their sides and she waits, and she watches the gap close up and we drive our spears deep into their bellies.

FAN. Why... why d'you kill them?

THE FATHER. Why did we kill them? For our waters, for the fish, because we always have done... why did she die? Because she turned back for them, because she didn't have the mind to know when the thing she loved would be the thing that did for her. (*Beat.*) How would you like to be The Daughter this year, dear little Fan?

FAN *is shocked; she looks to* JOSHUA.

FAN. The Daughter? But we haven't danced yet, I –

JOSHUA. You could do that for her? Choose her, like that?

THE FATHER *smiles at* JOSHUA *as if this is a ridiculous question.*

THE FATHER. There's none lovelier than you on the island, you have the spirit of The Daughter within you, the love you show for Maggie, the patience, and with all your sister has put you through, put all of you through, I think it could be just the thing to bring her back to us, what do you say? Come to the harbour with me and dance, and before them all, before the village, I'll place the crown on your head and name you Daughter. If the village see you. See you sat there before us all, loved by those around them, surely then, surely things must change... And if Maggie won't see sense, if she's intent on causing whatever damage she can, we all must let her go before she pulls us all into that black water with her.

JOSHUA. I'm happy to bring her down when the time is... I think the both of us would like to... Harsh words we had, Father, after you left, and I'd like to go and find her, try and bring her to the dance if she will –

THE FATHER. A blessed pure creature, this one.

FAN *is torn.*

FAN. For Maggie, I... Maybe I could go and find her, if I ask her, I shouldn't mind not being The Daughter if it meant we could all be there –

THE FATHER. You need to know when the thing you love is the thing that could do for you, little Fan. Am I right, Joshua?

Beat.

FAN. Da?

JOSHUA *swallows hard, looking at* THE FATHER.

JOSHUA. She's... her sister is all she's...

THE FATHER *walks to* JOSHUA *and towers over him, placing a thick arm around his shoulder. The threat is clear.*

THE FATHER. Is there a question in your mind, Joshua, that you aren't asking? If so, you need to speak up now, you need to let it be heard.

JOSHUA *is silent.*

No? So be it, the girl needs to go to the water. Collect your things.

FAN. Da?

JOSHUA *looks to* THE FATHER *but cannot hold his gaze. He looks back to* FAN, *a thin smile pasted across his face.*

THE FATHER. Come on, girl, listen to your da, the boats are ready for you, we need to leave.

FAN *looks at her father.* JOSHUA *kisses her head.*

FAN. Tell Maggie... can you tell her, the riddle, I think I understand, I know the answer.

JOSHUA. I... I'll tell her. Good girl, Fan. I'll find her, bring her down, I'm sure if she sees you... You look so pretty, Fan.

FAN. Goodbye, Da.

JOSHUA. Fan...

He looks at FAN *and then to* THE FATHER, THE FATHER'*s stare is steel. Whatever doubt he has* JOSHUA *dismisses.*

You look beautiful, my girl.

He straightens the flower crown on her head and kisses her on the cheek.

Go on, girl...

THE FATHER *and* FAN *turn and walk from the house.* JOSHUA *watches them go.*

Blackout.

Scene Six

Harbour wall.

GRETCHEN *is sat still and alone and silent, eyes closed. There is something dreamlike about her, like a mermaid on a rock. She sits for a moment before* MAGGIE *enters looking for her.*

MAGGIE. Gretchen! I've... you weren't at home, I've been looking all over for you.

GRETCHEN. Just a walk, no need to fuss.

MAGGIE. You need to come with me, we haven't much time, it must be nearly ten.

GRETCHEN. Come where, I can't... I need to rest, to –

MAGGIE. There's no time, please, Gretchen, I need your help, for Fan, for the other girls. The dance, it's started. The village are down by the harbour, they won't believe me on my own. I need your help. I need you to come with me, to show them, to tell them! Fan's there, Gretchen, Fan's going to dance and I know he'll pick her, to control me or scare me or... please, it can't happen again, not to her.

GRETCHEN. I don't... not now, Maggie, I don't want to go, with all those people there. All those eyes staring at me. Not now.

MAGGIE. Gretchen, please, I need your help. I know what happened. What happened to you, what he did to you on the boats. Listen, if we went together, to someone, anyone, someone who'll listen.

This frightens GRETCHEN.

GRETCHEN. And tell them what! We can't… what do you think we can tell them?

MAGGIE. The truth, what happened, the… if there's two of us.

Beat.

GRETCHEN. Why did you do that? Say I had to stay with you, at your house when he came. It was brave, I couldn't do that.

MAGGIE. Gretchen –

GRETCHEN. If it was you, if you were going with him and I was staying, I'm not sure I could have done that, I'd be too scared.

MAGGIE. We have no time, we need to go, to stop them.

GRETCHEN. Not now, please. I still don't think I'm fully well yet, my head is spinning and –

The weight of the day starts to catch up with MAGGIE, *we see the girl against the enormity of what she faces, a rowboat against the vast ocean.*

MAGGIE. It'll be too late, I need them to listen now.

GRETCHEN. I don't want them to see me.

MAGGIE. I know how scary it is, to speak to… but we must, Fan, the other girls, we have to –

GRETCHEN. I don't –

MAGGIE. We could tell them, warn them. (*Beat.*) That's why you were in the boat, why you got into trouble, isn't it, you were trying to leave the island, to escape.

GRETCHEN. Not leave.

MAGGIE. If we went together, if you could be brave, if you could come now, we still have time.

GRETCHEN. It won't change anything.

MAGGIE. I think we could.

GRETCHEN. Not for me.

MAGGIE. For others, for Fan... and maybe for us too, so we can start again.

GRETCHEN. It's too late, Maggie.

MAGGIE. No it's, they haven't rung the bell, it's not... we still have time.

GRETCHEN. It's gone. I don't want to go.

MAGGIE. They haven't rung the bells.

GRETCHEN. I want to go home.

> GRETCHEN *gets to her feet and turns to* MAGGIE. *As she stands we realise there is a large amount of blood on her skirt.* MAGGIE *sees the blood and jumps to her feet.*

I don't feel...

MAGGIE. Shit!

GRETCHEN. Please, I think I want to go home.

MAGGIE. You're bleeding where... oh shit.

> GRETCHEN *winces in pain.* MAGGIE *steadies her. Unnoticed at first,* JOSHUA *enters. His anger is quickly stayed when he sees the blood.*

GRETCHEN. I could feel it, inside me, I...

> GRETCHEN *touches her other hand to her stomach.*

Like a butterfly, like a fish in a bucket flipping and turning and I knew it was his... and I hated it, I hated it, and I hate him and I... I loved it... And I wanted to kill it, and I wanted to die.

MAGGIE. What's happened, Gretchen, what's... we can...

> MAGGIE *looks at her belly as it dawns on her.*

GRETCHEN. It was growing in my belly and I wanted…
I needed to go, to be gone… and this morning, I paddled
out, out from the harbour, like before, like when I was The
Daughter… my legs… I gathered the ropes together and
I wound them around my legs like some useless fishtail…

MAGGIE *holds her.*

MAGGIE. It's alright, you're alright.

GRETCHEN. I'm so scared, all the time I'm so scared and I
wanted it to stop. If he knew, if he found out, he's The Father,
if the village find out what will he do to me. We can't tell.

MAGGIE. It's, was it his? He… Oh God no! Gretchen, does he
still… is he still coming to you?

JOSHUA. What's happened, what's going on?

MAGGIE. Da! What are you doing here, where's Fan?

JOSHUA *stares.*

GRETCHEN. It's too late, it's gone.

JOSHUA *looks to* MAGGIE.

JOSHUA. Maggie, what's she talking about…?

MAGGIE. Are you still, are you bleeding?

GRETCHEN. It's stopped, it's gone.

JOSHUA. Whose baby, Maggie!?

MAGGIE. You know!

MAGGIE *looks at him.*

GRETCHEN. Please don't tell anyone, Mr Finn, please don't…

MAGGIE. Tell him about The Father, Gretchen.

GRETCHEN. You can't tell anyone please, Mr Finn.

JOSHUA. Have you made her… what have you told her,
Maggie.

GRETCHEN. It's not Maggie, it's… if he knows it was his.

JOSHUA. No!

MAGGIE. Look at her, Da, listen, you have to believe her.

JOSHUA. We barely know her.

MAGGIE. You know me! (*Beat.*) You know me, Da!

Beat.

JOSHUA. He did this to her?

Beat.

MAGGIE. To me.

Beat.

The weight of this starts to sink in.

To Fan maybe, if she's chosen.

This snaps JOSHUA *into focus.*

JOSHUA. If she's... she has been, he came back to the house...
She has been chosen. The Father said he'd put the crown on
her head, that she'd go out with the boats when the bells ring.

MAGGIE. Has she gone? Is she with him?

JOSHUA. I told her she'd be safe... I gave her to him.

Their gazes meet.

I'm... I never believed you. I thought she was safe.

MAGGIE. Come on, we need to go, if we run, if we hurry...

*She is cut off as the bells begin to ring, it is too late.
Everyone stops.*

No, Da!

GRETCHEN. The boats have sailed.

MAGGIE. Oh please, Da, no.

JOSHUA. It can't... he wouldn't... There might be time.

The bells are ringing, MAGGIE *looks to* JOSHUA, *the ships
have sailed.*

GRETCHEN. It's too late.

JOSHUA. There might be time, please, there might be…
  Please!

The lights fade. The bells swell in volume.

FAN *alone on stage.*

FAN. So that's why we dance… why we make the flower
  crowns and light the lanterns… the story goes that as The
  Daughter sank beneath the waves in the great jaws of the
  Orca they both disappeared… The storm stopped and the sea
  was still and as The Father pulled his nets in they were filled
  to bursting… the village was saved… I don't know if I
  believe it… all those stories… a girl is drowned, and
  everyone is saved… apart from they aren't… A girl is
  drowned…

Blackout.

The End.

A Nick Hern Book

Orca first published in Great Britain in 2016 as a paperback original by Nick Hern Books Limited, The Glasshouse, 49a Goldhawk Road, London W12 8QP, in association with Papatango and Southwark Playhouse, London

Orca copyright © 2016 Matt Grinter

Matt Grinter has asserted his right to be identified as the author of this work

Cover image: Rebecca Pitt

Designed and typeset by Nick Hern Books, London
Printed in the UK by Mimeo Ltd, Huntingdon, Cambridgeshire PE29 6XX

A CIP catalogue record for this book is available from the British Library

ISBN 978 1 84842 616 0